felt

26 PROJECTS FOR ALL FOR

frenzy

heather brack and
shannon okey

Interweave Press

Interweave Press LLC
201 East Fourth Street
Loveland, CO 80537-5655 USA
www.interweave.com

Printed and bound in China
through Pimlico.

Library of Congress
Cataloging-in-Publication Data

Brack, Heather, 1978-
  Felt frenzy : 26 projects for all
forms of felting / Heather Brack
and Shannon Okey, authors.
    p. cm.
  Includes index.
  ISBN-13: 978-1-59668-009-8
(pbk.)
  1. Felting. 2. Felt work. I. Brack,
Heather, 1978- II. Title.
  TT849.5.O44 2007
  746'.0463--dc22

  2006031040

10 9 8 7 6 5 4 3 2 1

To my Mom, who did everything and still inspires everything I do.
—Heather

To my aunt, Pat Hardy, who makes everything she does into art,
not just her paintings, and my mom, who's just like her.
—Shannon

acknowledgments

We couldn't have finished this book without the help of many wonderful friends and family members, among them Andi Moon Smith, who pinch-knitted for us more than once (all those swatchbar pieces? knitted by Andi); Kim Werker and Julie Holetz, for sharing their crochet knowledge; Susan Ensor, for keeping us company and relieving us on needlepunch duty while we made the green hat; Jana Stone, for thinking up and knitting the orange Bag of Many Pockets; Donna Pedaci, for being a friend and felting inspiration; Christine Okey (Shannon's mom), for doing much of the step-by-step photography and putting up with Shannon's type-A photo styling; Tamas Jakab, for working his Photoshop mojo; Jay Brack (Heather's dad) for never complaining about the yarn rats in the washing machine; Kim and Megan Brack (Heather's sisters) for field testing many of the patterns in this book; Bethany Banet and Chrissy Schwen, for helping in the best ways nonknitters know how; Susan Druding of Crystal Palace Yarns, for her fantastic yarn and all her inspiration; Jonelle Raffino of South West Trading Company, whose felted Karaoke sample at a 2005 TNNA show inspired our Karaoke wrap pattern; Matt Waldrup and Rob Matyska of Threadbear Fiber Arts, for keeping deep stock of every single color of Cascade 220 and encouraging Heather's early design efforts; Linda Diak of Grafton Fiber, for many gorgeous batts; Shannon's cats, who like to steal yarn and provide comic relief; and our dogs—Anezka, who occasionally stopped barking while we worked on the book, and Frankie, who ate too much of the wool floating around and coughed up felt, inadvertently creating a whole new technique. (Don't expect a chapter on *that*, though.)

All photos this page by Christine Okey

contents

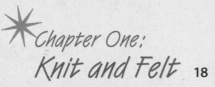

Foreword, or How We Got Started Felting